RIVERS THROUGH TIME

Settlements of the
INDUS
River

Rob Bowden

Heinemann Library
Chicago, Illinois

© 2005 Heinemann Library
a division of Reed Elsevier Inc.
Chicago, Illinois

Customer Service   888–454–2279

Visit our website at www.heinemannlibrary.com

Photo research by Ruth Blair and Ginny Stroud-Lewis
Designed by Richard Parker and Tinstar Design Ltd (www.tinstar.co.uk)
Printed in China by WKT Company Limited

09 08 07 06 05
10 9 8 7 6 5 4 3 2 1

Library of Congress Cataloging-in-Publication Data
Bowden, Rob.
  Settlements of the Indus River / Rob Bowden.
      p. cm. -- (Rivers through time)
  Includes bibliographical references and index.
  ISBN 1-4034-5718-2 -- ISBN 1-4034-5723-9 (pbk.)
1. Indus River--Juvenile literature. I. Title. II. Series.
  DS392.I5B68 2004
  954.91--dc22
                                    2004002421

Acknowledgments
The publishers would like to thank the following for permission to reproduce photographs:
Corbis p. 6, 30; Corbis pp. 26 (Stephanie Colasanti), 5 (Rik Ergenbright), 29, 35 (Hulton-Deustch Collection), 24 (Earl and Nazima Kowall), 23 (Galen Rowell), 36 (Nik Wheeler), 9 (Julian Woprker/Cordaiy); Christine Osborne pp. 8, 11, 13, 17, 18, 20, 27, 31, 41, 42; Ecoscene p. 39; Harappa p. 21 (Omar Khan); Link p. 12 (Dinoda); Panos Pictures p. 36 (Peter Barker), 33 (Neil Cooper), 32 (Daniel O'Leary), 11 (Chris Stowers); Still Pictures p. 25 (F. Vandersteenwinckel); Sylvia Cordiay p. 43; Trip p. 14 (R Graham), 37 (Pat Kerry)

Cover photograph reproduced with permission of Hutchinson/Juliet Highet.

Illustrator: Stephen Sweet (pp. 7, 10, 16, 28, 34, 38) Jeff Edwards (pp. 22)

Contents

Words in bold, **like this**, are explained in the Glossary.

Introducing the Indus River

A great river

The Indus is one of the world's greatest rivers. It stretches for a total distance of around 1,800 miles (2,900 kilometers) and carries twice as much water per year as the Nile, the world's longest river. But it is not just its geography that makes the Indus a great river. For thousands of years, the Indus River has been important to the people living in the surrounding lands. **Archaeologists** working in the Indus region have discovered the remains of ancient **settlements.** These show that the Indus was once home to a great **civilization,** known as the Indus valley civilization. Sometimes it is called the Harappan civilization after Harappa, one of the first settlements to be found. Archaeologists are still investigating the Indus valley civilization, but we know that it is over 5,000 years old and that the Indus River was key to its success.

The Indus is still very important to the people living alongside it today. This is particularly true for the people of Pakistan, because the Indus flows through the country for most of its length. Because of this, many of Pakistan's most important settlements are located along its banks. The Pakistani population of around 150 million people is almost completely dependent on the Indus, which provides water for farming, for industry, and for drinking.

River glossary

Confluence—the point where two rivers join.

Delta—where the river joins the sea.

Mouth—the ending point of a river.

Reaches—used to describe sections of the river (upper, middle, and lower reaches).

River course—the path followed by a river from source to mouth.

Source—the starting point of a river.

Tributary—a river or stream that joins another (normally bigger) river.

From source to mouth

The source of the Indus River is high on the Tibetan **plateau** in China. There, at an **altitude** of over 16,400 feet (5,000 meters), the Indus emerges from Lake Manasarovar. This is the start of the river's 1,800 mile (2,900 kilometer) journey to the Arabian Sea. In its upper **reaches,** the Indus is fed by **meltwaters** from the snowfields and glaciers of the Himalayas, the highest mountain range in the world, which it passes as it heads northwest into India. The Indus then continues through the mountains of northern India. As it crosses into northern Pakistan, it collects yet more meltwater from the Karakoram and Hindu Kush mountain ranges.

Swollen by all the meltwater, the narrow Indus is now a raging torrent. As it roars through the mountains, it carves some of the world's deepest **gorges.** The people of this region know the Indus as *Lion River*. According to legend, the Indus was born from the mouth of a lion and whoever drinks from it will become heroic, like a lion!

The Indus cuts narrow gorges through the mountains as it rushes to the sea.

The Indus has
the seventh
largest delta in
the world. It is
one and a half
times the size of
Israel and
almost three
times the size of
Jamaica!

This is a satellite
image of the Indus
delta, which covers
about 12,000
square miles
(30,000 square
kilometers).

Just to the east of Gilgit in northern Pakistan, the
Indus turns and heads southwest for the remainder of
its journey. At Kalabagh in northern Pakistan, the
Indus breaks free from the narrow mountain gorges.
Within 1 mile (1.5 kilometers), it slows down
dramatically and spreads out to around 10 miles (16
kilometers) wide. The Indus then flows gently through
the dry **plains** of central and southern Pakistan. It is
here that the Indus is a vital source of water for local
people. In this part of its journey, the Indus is joined by
five **tributaries**—the Jhelum, Chenab, Ravi, Beas, and
Sutlej rivers. These rivers give the region Punjab, which
means *land of five rivers*, its name. As it nears the
Arabian Sea, the Indus spreads out to form "the
mouths of the Indus." This is a giant **delta** that is 150
miles (240 kilometers) wide where it meets the sea.

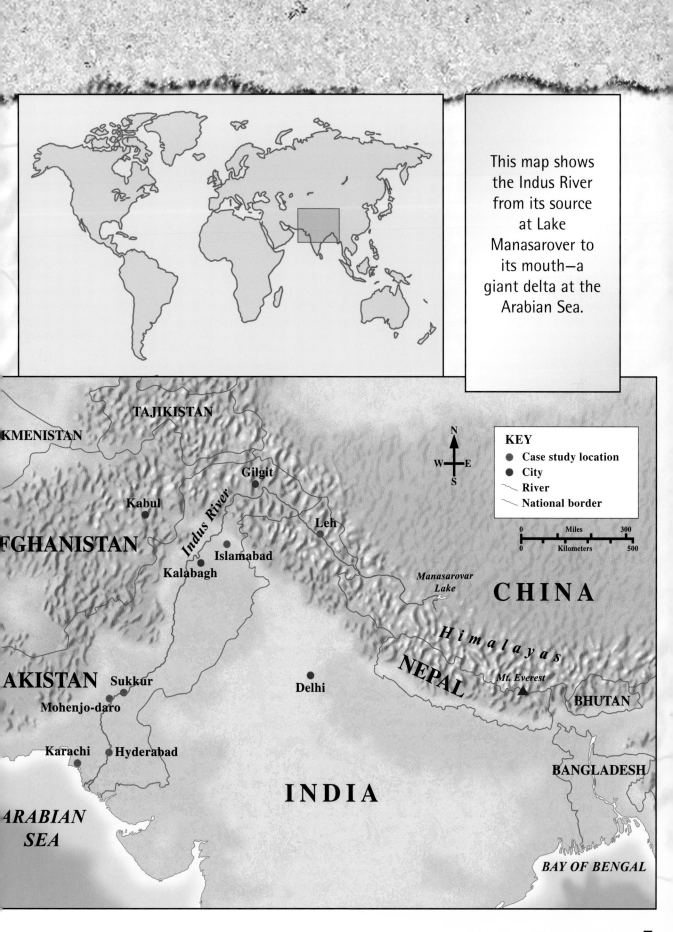

This map shows the Indus River from its source at Lake Manasarover to its mouth—a giant delta at the Arabian Sea.

KEY
● Case study location
● City
River
National border

0   Miles   300
0   Kilometers   500

TAJIKISTAN

KMENISTAN

Gilgit

Kabul

Indus River

Leh

AFGHANISTAN

Islamabad

Kalabagh

Manasarovar
Lake

CHINA

H i m a l a y a s

NEPAL

Mt. Everest

BHUTAN

AKISTAN

Sukkur

Delhi

Mohenjo-daro

Karachi   Hyderabad

BANGLADESH

INDIA

ARABIAN
SEA

BAY OF BENGAL

Settlements of the Indus

The type of land the Indus flows through determines the type of settlements that lie along its banks. Mountainous areas have little level ground to build on and have severe snow and ice for much of the year, cutting them off from the rest of the world. Despite these difficulties, there are a few key settlements here, such as Leh in northern India. These settlements have developed because of their locations on historic trade routes (see map on page 22). Merchants used these routes to transport goods between markets that were sometimes hundreds of miles apart. The upper Indus is on the trade route between China to the east and between Europe and the Middle East to the west.

Most of the Indus's settlements are along its middle and lower reaches. Here there is plenty of level land on which to build. The annual flooding of the Indus River has also created a valley rich in **nutrients.** These are carried down in the **sediment** from the mountains. The nutrient-rich soil is ideal for farming and has supported **agriculture** for thousands of years. Some villages along the Indus became busy markets that attracted people from great distances. Over time, they became important river settlements. Some have populations of over a million people today!

People settled in small villages along the Indus, living and farming in a similar way to the people who live there today.

The sprawling city of Hyderabad shows how rapidly some of the settlements along the Indus have grown.

In this book, we will explore some of the Indus's best-known settlements. We will follow a passage through time, starting with the ancient city of Mohenjo-daro. We'll end with the relatively modern city of Karachi, which is now one of the world's largest cities. We will look at why those settlements formed where they did and how they have changed over time. What are they like today, and how might they change in the future? Most importantly, of course, we will discover how the settlements are linked to the Indus. By looking at the settlements of the Indus and the people living there, we can see how the importance of the region and the river has changed over time.

What's in a name?

The origins of local names show the close ties between the Indus and the lands and people surrounding it. The country name India comes from Indus. Early records show that the Indus was originally known by its Sanskrit name, Sindhu. *Over time this changed under the influence of different languages, especially Arabic. Arabians pronounced* s *as* h *and so called the river and its people "Hindus".* Hinduism, *the name for the dominant religion in India, came from this. The river became known as the Indus, and India was used to describe the lands to the east of the Indus.*

Mohenjo-daro: City From the Past

Ancient secrets

Archaeologists have found the remains of about 1,500 ancient **settlements** in the Indus valley. This evidence shows that many settlements were small farming or fishing villages; however, some were larger, sophisticated cities. The largest of these cities was Mohenjo-daro. At the height of its development, Mohenjo-daro may have had a population of up to 40,000 people.

The ruins of Mohenjo-daro, dating from 2600 to 2500 B.C.E., were discovered in 1922 and are still being **excavated** today. While many of the excavated items provide us with a glimpse of what city life might have been like almost 5,000 years ago, some remain mysterious. For example, the local writing, which was similar to Egyptian hieroglyphics, is still not understood.

A gift of the Indus

Mohenjo-daro was very dependent on the Indus River. The annual flooding of the river created fertile **plains** on which peple easily grew wheat, barley, millet, fruit, and vegetables. The soil was so good that it produced a regular surplus, or extra amount, of food. This meant that people could do work other than farming. They could then trade their skills with the farmers in return for food.

Indus River

Mohenjo-daro

Sukkur

PAKISTAN

INDIA

This map shows the location of Mohenjo-daro today. The course of the Indus has changed over time and Mohenjo-daro is now almost a mile (about 1.5 kilometers away) from the river.

Over time, some people developed into highly skilled craftsmen who made pottery, cloth, jewelery, and leather goods. Other people began to trade these goods with people from as far afield as Mesopotamia (modern-day Syria and Iraq) and Egypt. The Indus was a vital transportation route for trade to the Arabian coast and beyond.

Pictures found at Mohenjo-daro show that such goods as grain, timber, and cotton were transported on a type of flat-bottomed boat. Similar boats are still used on the Indus today. The Indus also provided the people of Mohenjo-daro with fish to eat. Fragments of pottery that have been unearthed in the city clearly show images of nets, hooks, and different types of fish, some of which are still found in the river today.

Flat-bottomed boats can get close to the land, which makes it easy for loading. Today they are still used on the Indus to transport grain and other goods.

FACT

Mohenjo-daro means "mound of the dead" in English. Local people, who believed it was an ancient burial place, gave it its name. They may have been mistaken, however, because very few bodies have ever been found.

11

A planned city

Archaeologists have discovered that Mohenjo-daro was a very organized city. The whole city, including houses, neighborhoods and street networks, was carefully planned.

The city had two main parts, the **citadel** and the lower city. The citadel stands on a man-made earthen mound 40 feet (12 meters) above the surrounding flood plain. This provided protection from the regular flooding of the Indus. The citadel was in a good position for watching the city and river below. This may have helped the religious and political leaders, who probably lived there, to stay in power.

Water was very important in the city. The Great Bath is the most famous feature of the citadel. It could be the world's first-ever swimming pool! More likely, it was used for **ritual** bathing by people praying for a good harvest or for safety during the floods. The remains of what may be a granary also exist. Grain was an essential food source for the city, and the river provided the fertile land and means of transporting it. This proves just how vital the Indus was for the city.

This plan of Mohenjo-daro shows how well organized and how large the settlement was.

The Great Bath of Mohenjo-daro is one of the most famous buildings at the site.

The lower city makes up most of Mohenjo-daro. It is organized around a grid-pattern street network, similar to that of most U.S. cities. The main streets are up to 30 feet (9 meters) wide. Long ago, they would have been full of people and carts taking goods to and from the river. Narrower streets were built at right angles to the main streets. The doors to the houses were here, away from the dust and noise of the main street.

Archaeologists have excavated only a third of the lower city, but they believe it is divided into neighborhoods. There is a wealthy neighborhood where the houses are much larger. There is also an area where they think many of the skilled craftworkers lived.

Amazingly, Mohenjo-daro's houses had features that some settlements around the world still

FACT

The clay bricks that were used to build Mohenjo-daro are all exactly 11 in. by 5.5 in. by 3 in. (28 cm. by 14 cm. by 7 cm.). We know that children helped to make these bricks because of the small footprints found in them.

lack today. Many had their own private water supplies, with wells inside the houses. Bathrooms with paved-brick floors were also common. Waste water was taken away in a city-wide system of covered drains. These were frequently inspected and cleaned or repaired. Several houses had toilets that were separately emptied, and there were even neighborhood trash bins to help keep the streets clean.

A city in decline

For about 800 years, Mohenjo-daro was a thriving city. However, around 1800 B.C.E. it fell into decline and was soon abandoned. No one knows why this happened. The discovery of skeletons at the site has led some to believe that invaders stormed the city and killed many of the people. Or, the city may have declined after an earthquake changed the course of the Indus. Today, the Indus is almost a mile (about 1.5 kilometers) to the east of Mohenjo-daro. However, it used to flow just west of the city. Other rivers in the area dried up at this time, and the region is much drier than it used to be. This would have changed the pattern of flooding, severely affecting farming and trade along the Indus.

From the past to the present

Despite the city's decline, there are obvious links between the city of 5,000 years ago and that of today. The design of some boats has changed little, and carts used by riverside farmers today are almost identical to children's toys discovered at the ancient city.

The ruins at Mohenjo-daro attract many tourists every year.

c.3300 B.C.E.	c.2600 B.C.E.	c.2600–1800 B.C.E.	c.1800 B.C.E.
Small villages are established in the area around Mohenjo-daro.	Building of a planned city is begun at Mohenjo-daro.	Mohenjo-daro is a thriving trade city.	Mohenjo-daro falls into decline and is later abandoned.

Silt in the Indus can raise the water table and make flooding worse. Farmers haul the silt for the government and are able to keep it to use on their farms.

Boats even carry similar cargo, such as pottery and crops. Many of the skilled crafts that made Mohenjo-daro so impressive are still practiced in Pakistan and India. They include beadwork, pottery, jewelery, tilework, and weaving. In these ways, the Indus valley civilization survives in the lives of the people living there today.

Saving Mohenjo-daro

*Modern farming activities now threaten the ruins of Mohenjo-daro. **Irrigation** that uses water from the Indus has raised the **water table** under the city. As the water nears the surface, it brings salts with it. The salts slowly disintigrate, or break down, the clay bricks of Mohenjo-daro.*

Since 1972, the Pakistani government has been working with the international community to prevent such damage. A number of wells now pump water away from the foundations of the city. The government has banned farming in the area, and it has been trying to change the course of the Indus's waters to reduce the risk of flooding.

Unfortunately, parts of the city have already begun to disintegrate. These parts are now being capped with mud to prevent them from crumbling further. In a way, the ancient city of Mohenjo-daro is still locked in a battle with the Indus. The river that created the city may also be responsible for its destruction.

1922 c.e.	1948	1973	1980
Mohenjo-daro's ruins are discovered.	First attempts to conserve Mohenjo-daro are made.	Plans are approved to preserve Mohenjo-daro.	Mohenjo-daro becomes a World Heritage Site.

Sukkur: The Great Barrage

Shifting waters

For centuries, people living along the Indus have relied on its waters. However, sometimes the river brought them great hardships. Some hardships, such as floods submerging parts of local villages and towns, did not last long. Occasionally, though, the Indus undergoes major changes that seriously disrupt the lives of people living along it. One such change happened around 962 C.E., when an earthquake caused the Indus to shift to its present-day channel. **Settlements** that once thrived on the banks of the Indus were stranded, sometimes several miles from the river. This happened to the ancient city of Aror, the ruins of which now lie 5 miles (8 kilometers) to the east of the Indus.

The people of Aror relocated and established a settlement alongside the new course of the Indus. This new settlement became the modern-day city of Sukkur. By the 1200s, Sukkur, along with Rohri (on the opposite bank of the Indus), had a bustling port and was a center for trading local agricultural produce. Sukkur's vegetable market remains one of the city's most lively attractions.

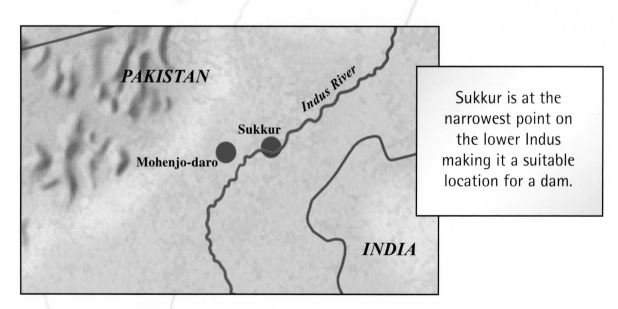

Sukkur is at the narrowest point on the lower Indus making it a suitable location for a dam.

Taming the Indus

Farmers in the Indus valley have always relied on the annual flooding of the river to provide the land with **nutrients** and water. Large parts of the valley receive very little rainfall, and without the waters of the Indus it would not be possible to grow crops. The problem with natural flooding is that it can be very unreliable. Sometimes the floods bring too much water, and sometimes they do not bring enough. Trying to predict when the floods will arrive is also a problem. Therefore, food production along the Indus valley has been unstable.

In the 1840s, the British took control of the area around Sukkur (known as Sindh) as part of the **British Empire.** They realized that if they could control the waters of the Indus then more food could be grown. By 1847 they had made up a plan to tame the river by building a **barrage** across it. The barrage would allow the waters of the Indus to be stored and released slowly to water the fields of Sindh throughout the year.

Sukkur was chosen as the site for this barrage. As the narrowest point in the lower Indus, it was an obvious location to try to dam the river. The British planned the Sukkur barrage but did not begin building it until 1923. It took almost ten years to build. When it was finished in 1932, the flow of the Indus was controlled for the first time.

At 4,650 feet (1,418 meters) in length, the Sukkur barrage is one of the largest dams in the world.

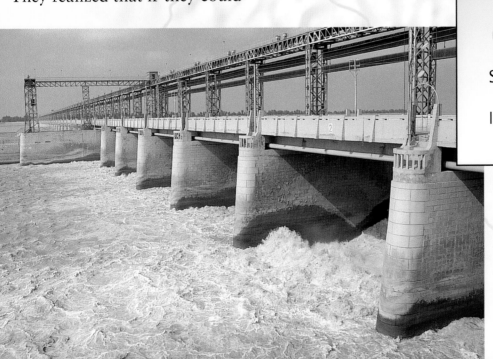

A giant water spider

The Sukkur barrage was built to change the flow of Indus waters to **irrigate,** or water, **uncultivated** land around Sukkur. Irrigation is widely used in areas with low rainfall. Seven canals were built to carry water from Sukkur to new areas of land. Four canals stretch out to the west, and three stretch to the east. From above they look like the legs of a giant seven-legged spider, with each canal creeping out into the land beyond. At the time it was built, the Sukkur irrigation system was the greatest in the world.

Irrigation canals like this carry water from the Sukkur barrage to the surrounding area.

It remains one of the world's largest systems today, with around 47,000 miles (75,000 kilometers) of canals irrigating close to 7.5 million acres of land.

Crops on the irrigated land are grown to meet the needs of local residents and to sell as cash crops. Local crops include a wide variety of vegetables and fruits. The area is particularly well known for its good bananas. The main cash crops include cotton, rice, sugarcane, and wheat.

A commercial center

Today, Sukkur is a major commercial center for the trading and processing of **agricultural** produce. For example, raw cotton is taken to Sukkur to be made into thread. The thread is then used in local textile factories to make cloth and clothing. Other industries process different crops grown in the area. These include flour and rice **milling** and the manufacture of sweets from sugarcane. Sukkur is particularly well suited as a commercial center. This is because it has good road and rail connections, which allow trade with other parts of Pakistan and neighboring Afghanistan. The road and rail bridges that cross the Indus in Sukkur are among the most important trade routes in Pakistan. The bridges can span the river here because the distance is made shorter by Bukkur Island, which lies in the middle of the river.

The excellent transportation connections and water supply have attracted new industries to Sukkur, such as **tanneries,** metalworking, and the manufacture of cement and chemicals. Though it is less important today, the river also continues to play a role in transporting raw materials and finished goods between Sukkur and settlements lower down the Indus. As Sukkur's commercial importance has grown, its population has grown as well. At the time the barrage was completed, there were fewer than 60,000 people living in Sukkur. However, by 2000 the city was home to 330,000 people—more than five times as many!

FACT

The Indus River system provides water that irrigates between 80–90 percent of Pakistan's farmland. The remaining farmland relies on rainfall.

An uncertain future

The Sukkur barrage was the first to be built across the Indus, but there are now several others. Most are located upstream of Sukkur, on the Indus or on one of its **tributaries.** Taking water from these barrages to irrigate crops has reduced the amount of water that reaches Sukkur. This has caused major problems for Sukkur's irrigation system. Recently, some of the canals have had to be closed. Others have been able to provide only half the normal amount of water. The water shortage is also affecting Sukkur's agricultural economy. If it continues, many people could lose their jobs or be foreced to leave the city to work somewhere else. The problem is caused partly by poorly maintained canals. Leakages cause the loss of up to 70 percent of the water, which never even reaches the fields. If the canals are improved and maintained, water could be used more efficiently. Changes are needed if Sukkur is to continue to thrive in the future.

The Lansdowne Bridge, built over the Indus at Sukkur in 1888, allowed trains to travel from Karachi to the north more easily.

962 c.e.	**c.1250**	**c.1842**	**1847**
Sukkur is founded.	Sukkur is established as a busy port.	British gain control of Sukkur.	First plans are made for a barrage at Sukkur.

The Mohana boat people

The Mohanas are a group of people who live on boats along the Indus and on nearby Manchar Lake. It is believed that the Mohanas have lived like this for thousands of years and may date back to the time of Mohenjo-daro. They live in village groups of five to ten boats. Each boat, which is called a *teen*, is divided into separate living areas and houses a family of six to ten people.

The Mohanas use reeds and other plants, such as the lotus flower, for food and to make goods, such as woven reed mats. The Mohanas fish and hunt waterfowl, but in a rather unusual way! They wade into the water with a stuffed egret (a bird similar to a heron) on their heads to trick the other birds. This allows them to get close enough to grab them.

Today, the Mohanas are found mainly on Manchar Lake, even though since the 1970s the government has tried to settle them along the Indus. Pollution in the waters of the Indus and Manchar now threatens their livelihood. Fish catches have fallen dramatically, and fewer birds are found in the area. More recently, the Mohanas' unique way of life has begun attracting tourists.

1888	1923	1932
Lansdowne Rail Bridge is built across the Indus at Sukkur.	Construction of Sukkur barrage begins.	Sukkur barrage is opened.

Leh: Mountains and Monasteries

Highland trading

Leh is the capital of the Ladakh region of northern India. Rock carvings in the region show that people have lived there for thousands of years. Early inhabitants would have been nomadic tribespeople. Nomads live on the move, traveling through their region in search of fresh grass for their animals, which include goats, sheep, and yaks. Some people still live this way today.

The first permanent **settlements** in the area developed as centers of trade connected to the famous Silk Road. This was an overland trade route that connected China with the Middle East and Mediterranean Europe. It is thought to have first developed around the 6th century B.C.E. and was the major trade route across Asia for about 1,500 years. The Indus and its **tributaries** created a path through the mountains. As one of the few accessible routes in the region, it introduced new peoples to the upper Indus.

This map shows the borders and country names when the Silk Road trade route was at its height. Leh developed as a settlement because of this trade route.

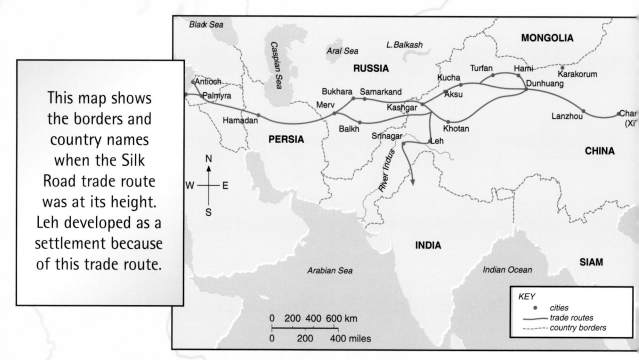

22

Terraced fields have been built into the mountainous regions of the upper Indus.

Around 900 C.E., the Thi dynasty took control of the region. The first dynasty to develop here, it ruled much of the Ladakh region from a capital built at Shey on the banks of the Indus. **Buddhism** spread into the region from neighboring Tibet. Over a hundred Buddhist monasteries, known as *gompas*, were built. Many of the gompas were located on the flatter land along the Indus. Leh, the current capital of Ladakh, was founded during the 1500s by Soyang Namgyal. He was a great leader who is famous for uniting the people of Ladakh into a single kingdom. He moved the capital from Shey to Leh, as it was closer to the Silk Road, the main trade route into China.

A hostile environment

The Ladakh region is a very hostile environment. However, settlements do exist there. The area receives little rainfall and becomes bitterly cold during the long winters, with temperatures of -16 °F (-30 °C) or lower. Between November and April, much of the region is completely cut off because of snow and ice. The areas of level land along the Indus and its tributaries provide some of the few places where people can settle, grow crops, and build houses. The people living here have also learned how to tap the **meltwater** that flows from the surrounding mountains to the Indus. Small streams run through the town of Leh and carry this precious water to the fields and houses.

23

Treasured kingdom

Leh is located just off the main Indus valley on a **plateau** watered by melting glaciers in the Himalayas. This means that there is enough water to grow wheat, barley, peas, and various vegetables to feed the people who live there. Its position on the trade route between India and China guaranteed Leh's status as a mountain **trading post** and helped it develop. Merchants from Tibet, India, Pakistan, and China would stop in Leh to trade in tea, salt, spices, semi-precious stones, and household goods. One of Leh's most valued goods was cashmere. Cashmere wool is famous for its softness and warmth. It comes from the fleece of Himalayan goats reared in the mountains around Leh.

Leh's importance in the world of trade caused several invading armies to try to capture it over the years. In 1834, general Zorawar Singh captured Leh for the Maharajah (prince) of Kashmir to gain control of the city's valuable cashmere trade. Leh's king fled and built a new palace at Stok, about 6 miles (10 kilometers) south of Leh. In the mid-1840s, Leh became part of the British Empire. It remained under British control before becoming part of independent India in 1947.

The palace of Leh, damaged during the invasion of Zorawar Singh in 1834, can still be seen today.

From trade to tourism

In 1950, disputes between India and China led to the closing of the Chinese border. This meant that Leh was no longer a major trade center. Many of Leh's residents found new jobs as workers for government road-building programs. The roads followed the Indus and linked Leh to settlements in the rest of India.

Leh had a lot to offer to India's growing tourist industry. The new roads meant people could reach Leh fairly easily, although they could still be blocked by snow and ice for half of the year. Even so, Ladakh was officially opened for tourism in 1974. Within a few years, Leh had become a favorite place for tourists to visit in northern India.

The fast-flowing waters of the upper Indus offer some of the world's best white water rafting. Many tourists use Leh as a base for rafting expeditions.

Leh's main attractions are its Buddhist history and its beautiful river and mountain scenery. Many tourists are interested in the gompas, the Buddhist monasteries that line the Indus and its tributaries. Others come simply to enjoy the mountain environment and hike along the Indus paths, just as merchants would have done in the past. More recently, the Indus has become popular for white-water rafting. This allows tourists to see the river up close and to challenge themselves in its swirling and crashing waters.

Impact of tourism

The number of tourists visiting Leh has increased
steadily since 1974. Jobs and money from the tourist
industry attracted local people to move to the city,
and this caused a dramatic population increase.
Between 1975 and 2000, Leh's population more than
doubled to around 27,500 people. Leh has grown to
meet the demands of tourism. An airport was built to make it
easier for people to reach Leh. This has increased tourist
numbers even more. Between 1998 and 1999, Leh airport
handled about 90,000 passengers. This is several times more
than the number of people that live in the city itself.

Hotels and hostels were opened in Leh to accommodate tourists.
Other services, such as restaurants and gift shops, have also
grown. Many of these are run by non-Ladakhi people from

Most tourists arrive
in Leh by plane,
but some come
by car along
the roads that
follow the course
of the Indus.

900	c.1550	1834
First settlements are established in the area around Leh.	Leh is founded as the new capital by Seyang Namgyal.	Zorawar Singh captures Leh for the Maharaja of Kashmir.

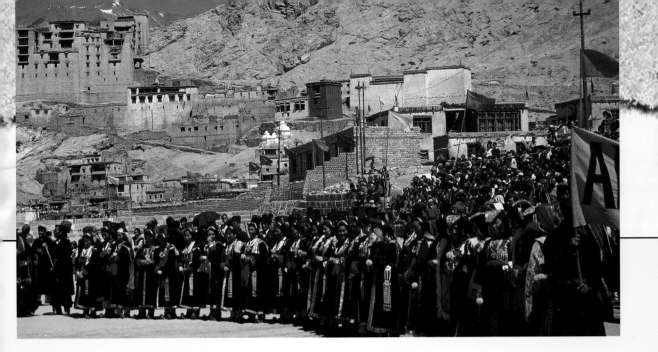

The gompas of Ladakh

Dotted along the upper **reaches** *of the Indus as it passes through Ladakh are several Buddhist monasteries known as* gompas. *Gompas are normally built on high ground, overlooking the river valleys below. They have been places of worship for hundreds of years and are still in use today. Many contain historical Buddhist artworks such as face masks, religious costumes, and painted or embroidered scrolls, known as* thangkas. *Several of the gompas hold annual festivals to celebrate different aspects of the Buddhist religion. These attract people together from settlements across the region.*

Kashmir. Leh's tourist activities are placing enormous pressure on its environment. Mountain streams supplying water to Leh's agricultural fields have been running low because water is taken for tourists to use. Some of this water is used for western-style flush toilets. These have caused an additional problem: leaking sewage pollutes local streams and rivers, such as the Indus. Traditionally, people in Leh use compost toilets which do not pollute or use valuable water. Waste disposal has also polluted some local water supplies. The Ladakh Ecological Development Group was established in 1984 to tackle these problems. It encourages local people and tourists to think more carefully about Leh's fragile mountain environment. It wants people to enjoy Leh's historic sites and the Indus valley, but to also preserve them for future generations.

1840s	1974	1984
Leh becomes part of British-controlled India.	Leh is opened to international tourism.	Ladakh Ecological Development Group is established to protect Leh.

Hyderabad: The Crossroads

An ideal location

Hyderabad is located on a hill on the east bank of the Indus. This is an ideal location for a **settlement.** The river provides settlers with a regular water supply and is a natural transportation route to neighboring settlements. Hyderabad's location on a hill provides a lookout over the surrounding **plains.** It also provides safety and protection from invading forces. The benefits of Hyderabad's location have long been recognized. Its ancient name, Nerun Kot, refers to a Hindu ruler named Nerun, who built a fort, or kot, there. Hyderabad continues to be a **strategic** location. However, today it is important as a center for transportation and communications rather than for military defense.

Born from the river

The modern city of Hyderabad was founded in 1768 after a gradual change in the course of the Indus. In around 1758, the Indus flooded the capital of the Sindh region at Khudabad. Ghulam Shah Kalhora, the ruler of Sindh, set out to find a new site for his capital city. He decided on the site that is now Hyderabad and built a fort on the hill that still stands today.

FACT

With a length of 1.25 miles (2 kilometers), the Shahi Bazaar in Hyderabad is one of the longest in Pakistan.

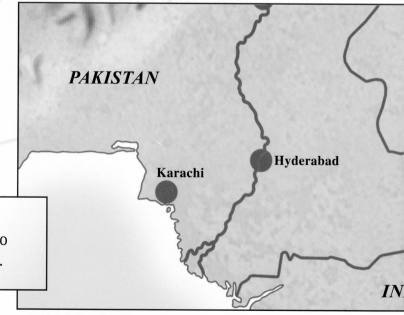

The modern city of Hyderabad is located close to its ancient hill-top position.

This shows the main bazaar (market) in Hyderabad in the early 1900s. The Char Minar arch at the end dates back to 1591.

The new settlement was named after the prophet Mohammed's son-in-law, Ali, also known as Haidar. In 1782 to 1783, Hyderabad came under the control of the Talpurs, a tribe from western Pakistan. They kept Hyderabad as the capital of Sindh and continued to develop the city.

The Sindh region produced a bounty of food every year, thanks to the annual floodwaters of the Indus. Hyderabad became a busy market town where people traded farm produce for manufactured goods, such as textiles, household goods, and such luxury items as jewelery. As a result, Hyderabad became a center for expert craftspeople, and the central bazaar (market) became one of the most important in Pakistan.

River trade

As the British expanded their Indian colony into modern-day Pakistan, they were quick to recognize the benefits of the Indus. As early as 1809 they had begun to deal with the Talpur rulers in Hyderabad to gain passage up the Indus. In 1843 British forces, under Sir Charles Napier, defeated the Talpur army and seized control of Hyderabad. This also gave the British control of the Indus and the Sindh region, and marked the end of an era in Hyderabad. Although the city continued to be of great importance, it lost its title as capital of Sindh, as the British established a new capital in Karachi.

29

The electricity produced by the Kotri barrage helps support local industries.

Commercial center

The Indus River remains vitally important to the settlement of Hyderabad. It provides transportation to neighboring settlements and water for **agriculture,** industry, and domestic use. The Indus became increasingly important when the Kotri **barrage** was built just upstream of Hyderabad in 1955. This barrage provided **irrigation** water that more than doubled the area that could be farmed around Hyderabad. It also benefited the water-thirsty cotton industry. Pakistan is the world's fourth-largest producer of cotton, producing around nine percent of the world total in 2001–02. Hyderabad is in the middle of one of Pakistan's main cotton-producing areas, so the city has developed into a major cotton-processing center.

In turn, Hyderabad's cotton has made it a good location for the textile industry. The city is close to the raw material (cotton yarn), and has a plentiful supply of water. Textile production uses large amounts of water in the washing, dyeing, and bleaching processes, and so is often located along rivers.

FACT

Cotton first originated in Pakistan. It is now cultivated in 90 countries and is probably the most widely used fabric in the world.

The Kotri barrage also supplies electricity to Hyderabad. Electricity is produced as the Indus passes through generators in the barrage. The combination of electricity and water supplies has attracted several other industries to Hyderabad, including cement, leather, and paper manufacturers.

This is a cotton factory in Hyderabad. Water from the river is used to process and transport the cotton.

Industries are also attracted to Hyderabad's good transportation links. The city provides the main crossing point over the Indus for road and rail traffic traveling between Karachi, to the west, and Islamabad, to the east. Road and rails have replaced the river as the main transportation routes because they are considered more convenient and offer greater flexibility than the fixed route of the Indus does. The construction of barrages across the Indus has also reduced river transportation because they disrupt the **navigation** of the river.

Labor demand

Many people have moved to Hyderabad in search of work in the city's growing industries. Others have found work providing services for the industrial workers, such as stores, banks, restaurants, transportation, and recreation companies. As a result, the city has grown rapidly over the last fifty years. It is gradually spreading outward as new housing is built. Between 1961 and 2000, the population of Hyderabad more than doubled, reaching around 1.2 million people. Pakistan has one of the highest population growth rates in the world, so Hyderabad will continue to expand even if no more people move to the city. By 2015, Hyderabad's population is expected to be around 1.9 million.

Badghirs

Hyderabad's climate is hot for much of the year, but people have developed an ingenious way of cooling down their houses. During the hot summer months, a cool breeze blows from the southwest, up the Indus delta toward Hyderabad. In order to benefit from this breeze, people have constructed badghirs *on their roof tops. Badghirs look a little like chimneys but have open slats that allow the cool breeze to enter and pass into the house below.*

Environmental pressures

Hyderabad is one of the biggest cities on the Indus, and it contributes more to the environmental pressures on the river than many others do. Large volumes of water are extracted for industry and farming. Waste from farmers' fields, households, and such industries as **tanneries,** textiles, and paper-making is dumped in the Indus. The waste water from industries is often fed back into the Indus without any treatment, even if it contains chemicals and heavy metals. This waste pollutes the river and is dangerous for local wildlife and people using the water farther downstream.

The use of chemicals in farming has led to higher levels of water pollution in the Indus River.

Agriculture also causes water pollution. Farmers use chemicals such as **pesticides** and fertilizers to help their crops grow. Some of these chemicals mix with irrigation or rain water and end up back in the Indus. The chemicals can pollute the river water and kill local plant and animal life. The river water can also become unsafe for human beings to drink. If people continue to drink heavily polluted water, they can become seriously ill or even die.

1768	1782–83	c.1809
Hyderabad is founded as the capital of Sindh by Ghulam Shah Kalhora.	Hyderabad is taken over by the Talpurs from Baluchistan.	British negotiate with Hyderabad Talpurs to use the Indus.

A woman collects water from the Indus. Many people rely on the untreated waters of the Indus to meet their household water needs.

One of the biggest causes of water pollution is the poor treatment of human sewage from settlements along the Indus. Most sewage finds its way back into the river untreated, or treated at a very basic level. It can easily **contaminate** drinking water supplies with water-borne diseases. If contaminated water is used to irrigate crops, the food supplies can beome contaminated too. Water-borne diseases kill 10 percent of Pakistani children before they reach the age of one. Overall, polluted water is blamed for around 40 percent of all deaths in Pakistan. Hyderabad has a high risk of water pollution because it receives the pollutants not only from settlements upstream but also from the city itself. In 2002, the Sindh Environmental Protection Agency launched a project to monitor water pollution in and around Hyderabad. This is seen as a first step to cleaning up the Indus.

Human beings have created environmental pressures along the entire length of the Indus. The **extraction** of water for human use is one of the biggest pressures because it reduces the amount of water in the river. The main impact is felt in the lower **reaches** of the Indus, south of Hyderabad. In addition, as settlements expand, land on both sides of the river is being converted either to farmland or housing. This causes a loss of the river habitat and of wildlife that once lived there. Pollution also affects most of the river. As the settlements of the Indus grow larger in the future, these environmental pressures are expected to only get worse.

1843	1947	1955
British defeat the Talpur army and take control of Hyderabad.	Hyderabad becomes part of newly independent Pakistan.	Kotri barrage is built just upstream of Hyderabad.

Karachi: A Mega-City

Humble beginnings

Today, Karachi is one of the world's twenty biggest cities. However, it started out as a quiet fishing village called Kalachi-jo-Goth. Located at the northern end of the vast Indus **delta,** Karachi was surrounded by a collection of islands among the delta's **mangrove swamps.** The area also had a natural harbor bordering the Arabian Sea. It was this harbor that first attracted people to build a settlement at Kalachi-jo-Goth.

The Talpurs gained control of the land around Karachi at the end of the 1700s and built a simple mud fort to protect the harbor and fishing village. The village soon grew into a small town, and by 1818 it had a population of around 13,000 people. The arrival of the British launched the development of Karachi, with Sir Charles Napier declaring, "One day she [Karachi] will be the Queen of the East."

Connection to the world

By 1843, British control had spread to Hyderabad and the entire Sindh region. The British saw that Karachi was important for controlling trade on the Indus, and moved the capital of Sindh from Hyderabad to Karachi. Troops were brought in to protect

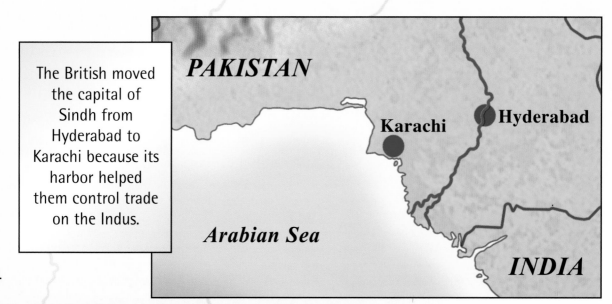

The British moved the capital of Sindh from Hyderabad to Karachi because its harbor helped them control trade on the Indus.

This shows goods being transported from East Pakistan to West Pakistan through the harbor at Karachi in 1956.

the region, and Karachi grew as traders arrived to provide the army with services and goods. An administrative district was also established to manage not just Karachi, but all of Sindh. The British also developed Karachi's port, allowing the trade of Sindh's agricultural riches to reach the rest of the world.

The British set up river transportation companies such as the Indus Steam Flotilla and the Orient Inland Steam **Navigation** Company. These companies brought farm produce, such as wheat, down the Indus, through the delta and into Karachi's port. The main crop, cotton, was shipped from Karachi to the textile mills of Great Britain.

River trade on the Indus was soon booming, and after just eighteen years of British control the value of goods traded from Karachi had increased sevenfold to £855,103 in 1856. The great wealth to be made in the Indus region attracted British companies and merchants who set up offices and warehouses in Karachi. In turn, Karachi's population grew, as people came to take advantage of new job opportunities. It had reached around 57,000 by 1856.

The boom years

Between 1861 and 1865, during the U.S. Civil War, Harachi's development received an unexpected boost from the United States. The war severely disrupted the supply of cotton from U.S. plantations to the textile mills of Great Britain. Searching for an alternative source of cotton, British cotton producers turned to Karachi and the cotton of the Indus. In 1861, the Sindh railway was built, connecting Karachi to the cotton- and wheat-growing areas around Hyderabad and Kotri. When the railroad was extended in 1869, it connected it further into the cotton-growing regions of Punjab to the north. This dramatically increased the trade passing through Karachi. As the country's leading sea port, Karachi was further helped when the Suez Canal opened in 1869 to connect Europe to Asia. It made Karachi the country's closest port to Great Britain.

Karachi handles an incredible 95 percent of all Pakistan's foreign trade.

By 1872, the value of trade passing through Karachi had reached more than $5 million a year, and this brought great wealth to the city. The port was modernized to cope with the growth in trade. In addition, many of Karachi's finest buildings, which were often very British in style, were built during this period. For example, Empress Market, a thriving fruit and vegetable market, was built to resemble the market halls found in north England during the mid-1800s.

Still thriving

Karachi has continued to thrive as a city ever since. When Pakistan became independent in 1947, Karachi remained the capital until Islamabad was chosen to replace it in 1958. Although it lost its status as capital, Karachi has remained the most economically important city in Pakistan. This is because of its favorable position as the gateway to the Indus valley. Today, it handles a wide variety of goods from across Pakistan, though cotton is still a major export. The river plays less of a role in the transportation of goods today. However, the Indus is still vital to Karachi's development because it supports many businesses and industries relied upon for the city's trade. The people who live in Karachi also rely on the Indus as a source of drinking water.

Today, in Pakistan, goods are often transported by road in trucks like these rather than by river.

Rapid growth

Karachi needed a plentiful supply of workers to help build the city and run the rapidly growing port. As a result, people came by the thousands from other parts of India and elsewhere. The city expanded rapidly. The growing population increased the demand for goods and services. This, in turn, increased the demand for workers. More people arrived, hoping to share in the wealth being made in Karachi. Some set up their own businesses. Between 1901 and 1941, Karachi's population grew by 300,000 to reach 436,000 people. This is the same as just over 20 people arriving in the city every day and never leaving!

This increase in population was set to continue. In 1947, Pakistan and India gained their independence from Britain. They had both been part of one large British colony, but when they became independent, they divided to form two new countries. This division was known as the **partition**. Before partition, Karachi had attracted people from all over India. It had a mixed population of about 51 percent Hindu and 42 percent Muslim.

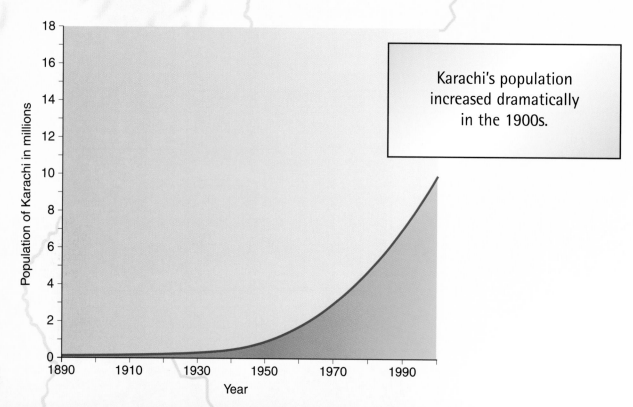

Karachi's population increased dramatically in the 1900s.

This village in the Indus delta region has been abandoned where salt in the water has made the land useless.

During partition a mass migration took place. Hindus moved to the mainly Hindu country of India, and Muslims from India moved to Pakistan, which was mainly Muslim. Most of Karachi's Hindu population **emigrated,** but the city gained at least 600,000 Muslim **immigrants.** The population of Karachi more than doubled in just four years to reach more than a million people by 1951. The mix of Karachi's population also changed to around 94 percent Muslim and just 2 percent Hindu. Ever since partition, Karachi's population has continued to expand at an incredible rate. More and more people arrive in the city on an almost daily basis.

Indus refugees

*Some of the more recent arrivals in Karachi have been people from the Indus delta region. The **extraction** of water further up the Indus has caused the amount of water reaching the Indus delta to fall drastically in recent decades. This is now having a major impact on the delta region and its people. As the Indus waters fall, sea water flows into the delta region to take its place—a process known as salt water intrusion. Sea water is saline (salty), but many of the crops and fish that were once harvested in the delta cannot survive in salt water. It has been estimated that 618,000 acres of agricultural fields have been lost due to salt water intrusion over the last 50 years. With their livelihoods threatened or lost, many farmers and fishermen have sought refuge with their families in nearby Karachi.*

Population overload?

One of the biggest problems in Karachi is that its infrastructure—which is made up of its roads, water supplies, and electricity—has not kept pace with population growth. Around 40 percent of Karachi's residents live in slum settlements, known as *katchi abadis*, located in and around the city. As the city continues to expand, many newcomers end up in these crowded slums. Others begin to build new slums on any available patch of land. This unplanned development has caused enormous problems, such as a lack of schools and hospitals, crowded and dirty streets, and growing crime. The problems have led experts to believe that the city is suffering from population overload.

Water pollution

Water pollution is a big problem in Karachi. Its sewerage system is inefficient, and the majority of homes are not even connected to it. Vast amounts of sewage are simply dumped into open channels and streams that flow into the Indus delta.

Open sewers run through the slums of Karachi. The sewage flows into the Indus.

c.1775–1800	1818	1839	1856	1861
Talpurs gain control of the land around Karachi.	Karachi develops into a small town.	British gain control of Karachi from the Talpurs.	Karachi becomes a busy port at the mouth of the Indus.	Railroad is opened connecting Karachi to Sindh province.

Fishermen here are sorting palla by size in Karachi. Pollution in the Indus has seriously affected the fishing industry.

Karachi's industries dump much of their waste water in a similar way. Ships visiting the port add to the pollution by dumping waste and spilling oil into the delta.

The Indus delta receives a constant mixture of raw sewage, toxic chemicals, and solid waste. This pollution affects not only the quality of water in the delta, but also the plants and animals that live there. Extraction of water upstream means that less fresh water reaches the delta. This causes polluting chemicals to build up in the delta region rather than being washed out to sea.

These problems have badly affected the fishing industry. The Indus delta provides about 70 percent of the coastal fish caught in Pakistan.

FACT

The population of Karachi's slums is said to be increasing by around 200,000 people per year!

As the delta worsens, so too does the fish catch. Between 1986 and 2001, the catch of two important fish species, the palla and dangri, fell by about two-thirds.

If Karachi is to continue growing, its government needs to introduce tighter controls on water pollution. Otherwise, the pollution will increase as Karachi's population does. Some scientists warn that the delta **ecosystem** could collapse altogether. This would cause thousands of people to lose their livelihoods and end up in the slums of Karachi.

1861–65	1869	1947	1958	c.1980 onwards
Karachi's cotton exports are boosted by the Civil War.	Railroad is extended from Karachi into Punjab.	Karachi becomes capital of newly independent Pakistan.	Islamabad replaces Karachi as the capital of Pakistan.	Refugees from the Indus delta move to Karachi.

The Indus of Tomorrow

Gifts of the Indus

All of the **settlements** described in this book exist because the Indus River flows through or past them. The Indus is a truly great provider. It brings life to a part of the world that would otherwise be a barren, virtually lifeless desert. Over the 5,000 years or so that people have settled along the river, they have learned how to control and manage the river for their own benefit. As the remains of Mohenjo-daro or the grand buildings of Karachi show, this has brought great wealth to the region.

Developments in technology allowed people to gain even greater control of the river. The Sukkur **barrage,** for example, enabled them to create an **irrigation** program on the Indus that remains the largest in the world. Progress in transportation opened up the Indus to new trading opportunities and led to the development of some of its largest cities in Hyderabad and Karachi. These cities continue to play a major role in world trade today.

Attempts are being made to care for the river environment of the Indus. An example is the planting of mangrove nurseries like this.

These workers are lining an irrigation canal near Sukkur. Lining canals improves their efficiency and will help to reduce pressure on the Indus.

Caring for the Indus

Unfortunately, human activities along the Indus have had a negative affect on the river. The Indus' settlements **extract** an increasing amount of water for their rapidly growing populations. They also generate a great deal of waste that is often untreated. Much of it is dumped back into the Indus, and this causes pollution and threatens life further downstream. The poor state of the Indus **delta** is a clear sign of the damage being done. Shortages of irrigation water also warn that too many demands are being placed on the Indus River.

Such measures as reducing industrial pollution or improving the efficiency of the irrigation network would help the situation. The problem for the Indus settlements, however, is their continuing population growth. By 2050, the population of Pakistan is expected to more than double to 345 million people. The majority of these people will live in settlements along the Indus and its **tributaries.** This increase in population will make it a major challenge to reduce demands being placed on the river. In the past, great civilizations have collapsed because they failed to take care of the river that provided for them. The people of the Indus valley have lived with the river for thousands of years. In the future, they must learn to protect the great Indus River, so that generations to come can benefit from its waters.

43

Timeline

c.3300 B.C.E.	Small villages are established in the area around Mohenjo-daro.
c.2600	Building of planned city begins at Mohenjo-daro.
c.2600–1800	Mohenjo-daro is a thriving trade city.
c.1800	Mohenjo-daro falls into decline and is later abandoned.
900 C.E.	First **settlements** are established in the area around Leh.
962	Sukkur is founded.
c.1250	Sukkur is established as a busy port.
c.1550	Leh is founded as the new capital of Ladakh.
1768	Hyderabad is founded as Sindh's capital.
1782–83	Hyderabad is taken over by the Talpurs from Baluchistan.
c.1809	British negotiate with Hyderabad Talpurs to use the Indus.
1818	Karachi develops into a small town.
1834	Zorawar Singh captures Leh for the Maharaja of Kashmir.
1839	British gain control of Karachi from the Talpurs.
c.1840s	Leh becomes part of British-controlled India.
c.1842	British gain control of Sukkur.
1843	British defeat the Talpur army and take control of Hyderabad.
1847	First plans are made for a **barrage** at Sukkur.
1856	Karachi becomes a busy port at the mouth of the Indus.
1861	Railroad is opened, connecting Karachi to Sindh province.
1861–65	Karachi's cotton exports are boosted by the American Civil War.
1869	Railroad is extended from Karachi into Punjab.
1888	Lansdowne Rail Bridge is built across the Indus at Sukkur.
1922	Ruins of Mohenjo-daro are discovered.
1923	Construction of Sukkur barrage begins.
1932	Sukkur barrage is opened.
1947	Sukkur, Hyderabad, and Karachi become part of newly independent Pakistan. Leh becomes part of independent India.
1948	First attempts are made to conserve Mohenjo-daro.
1955	Kotri barrage is built just upstream of Hyderabad.
1958	Islamabad is chosen to replace Karachi as capital of Pakistan.
1980	Mohenjo-daro becomes a **World Heritage Site.**
c.1980	Refugees from the Indus **delta** move to Karachi.
1984	Ladakh Ecological Development Group is established to protect Leh.

Further resources

Books

Country Profiles: Pakistan,
Khawar Mumtaz et al. Oxfam, 2003.

Excavating the Past: Indus,
Ilona Aronovsky and Sujata Gopinath. Heinemann Library, 2004.

Nations of the World: India,
Anita Dalal. Raintree, 2003.

Understanding People in the Past: The Indus valley,
Naida Kirkpatrick. Heinemann Library, 2002.

Using the Internet

Where to search
A search engine will look through the entire web and list all
the sites that match the words in the search box. Try
www.google.com. A search directory is a library of websites that
have been sorted by a person instead of a computer. You can
search by keyword or subject and browse through different
related sites. A good example is **yahooligans.com**.

Search tips
There are billions of pages on the Internet, so it can be difficult
to find exactly what you want. These search skills will help you
find useful websites more quickly:
• Use two to six simple keywords, putting the most
  important words first.
• Be precise, only use names of people, places or things.
• If you want to find words that go together, put quotation
  marks around them, for example "St Anthony's falls" or
  "Gateway Arch".
• Going to the "cached" option of a result will highlight where
  the keywords you searched for appear on the website.

Glossary

agriculture practice of growing crops or raising animals for food or to sell

altitude distance (or height) above sea level, measured in feet or meters

archaeologist someone who specializes in investigating the past from evidence that was left behind, usually found buried under ground

barrage artificial barrier that is normally built across a river to provide protection against floods or to produce hydroelectricity

British Empire period in which Britain had political and military control over large parts of the world. It was at its greatest between the early 1600s and the late 1800s.

Buddhism form of religion, particularly common in central Asia

citadel fortified building in or near a city, often where rulers lived

civilization an organized society

contaminate to make something become unclean. For example, water can be contaminated when it becomes polluted.

cultivated describes land that is farmed

delta area at the mouth of a river formed by the deposit of sand and soil in a triangular shape

ecosystem environment such as a pond, river, or forest, and all the animals and plants that live within it

emigrate to leave a place (normally a country) to live elsewhere

excavate to dig up or unearth something

extract to remove by force. Often used to describe the taking of water from a river.

fertilizers chemicals that are applied to crops to feed them and encourage growth

gorge natural cutting through a landscape formed by a river

immigrant person who arrives in a place (normally a country) from elsewhere

irrigation watering crops using specially created systems. Normally used in areas of low rainfall.

mangrove swamp form of forest that grows in shallow water around rivers or coastal areas in tropical countries

meltwater water that has melted from glaciers or ice fields in mountainous areas

milling conversion of raw material (such as wheat) into finished goods (such as flour)

navigation act of directing or moving a boat along a river or across a lake or sea

nutrients substances that provide food to plants or animals. Soils, for example, carry mineral nutrients that help plants to grow.

partition process by which Britain's Indian colony was divided into India and Pakistan at independence in 1947

pesticides chemicals used in farming to kill pests that can otherwise damage crops

pictorial using pictures instead of letters or words as a form of communication

plain wide, normally level, area of land often found to either side of a river in its middle and lower reaches

plateau level top of a hill or mountain

reaches part of a river's course. Rivers are normally divided into upper, middle, and lower reaches.

ritual ceremonial or traditional practice performed by people. Often associated with a religion, but can also be linked to specific cultures.

sediment soil-like material that is carried in water

settlement place that has people living in it permanently. Settlements can vary in size from a small village to a large city.

strategic vital part of a plan (strategy). For example, a bridge can be a strategic target in a military campaign.

tannery the name given to a place where animal skins are tanned as part of the leather-making process

trading post store or town (often in a remote location) where local produce is exchanged or sold for goods and supplies from elsewhere

tributary river or stream that joins another, normally larger, river

uncultivated land that has not been farmed

water table level under the ground below which the earth or rocks are filled with water. A water table can rise or fall over time.

World Heritage Site site of cultural or natural importance. In 2003, there were 754 World Heritage Sites.

Index